The BIG POD
Upload & Update Log
Indie Book Management

Book # _____

From: _____ to _____

WestWard Journals
WestWard Books
Payson, Arizona

WestWard Journals

Copyright © 2018 Marsha Ward

Cover Photo by Becca Lavin at Unsplash

ISBN-13: 978-1-947306-14-1

INTRODUCTION

This Log contains space to make note of upload and update details for twenty self-published print books. It is intended to be used for books printed by KDP Print, but probably is flexible enough for other POD services, too. It contains ample pages for notes about updates and changes, which should help keep track of any details the Indie or Self-Publishing Author and Publisher may need.

MY PROJECT IDEAS

_____

_____

_____

_____

_____

_____

_____

_____

_____

_____

_____

_____

_____

_____

_____

_____

_____

_____

_____

_____

MY BOOKS

Book 1   Title _____   Page 1
           _____

Book 2   Title _____   Page 9
           _____

Book 3   Title _____   Page 17
           _____

Book 4   Title _____   Page 25
           _____

Book 5   Title _____   Page 33
           _____

Book 6   Title _____   Page 41
           _____

Book 7   Title _____   Page 49
           _____

Book 8   Title _____   Page 57
           _____

Book 9   Title _____   Page 65
           _____

Book 10   Title _____   Page 73
           _____

BOOK 1 - Date _____

Paperback Details

Language _____

Book Title _____

Subtitle _____

Series _____ # ____

Edition Number (if it applies) _____

Author _____

Contributors (if any) _____

_____

_____

_____

Description: _____

_____

_____

_____

_____

_____

_____

_____

_____

_____

_____

_____

_____

_____

Publishing Rights (circle or underline one)

I own the copyright

This is a public domain work

1

Book Title _____

Keywords (seven words or phrases)

_____

_____

_____

_____

_____

_____

_____

Categories (two)

_____

_____

_____

_____

Large Print   No Yes

Adult Content   No Yes

Paperback Content

Print ISBN (circle one)   Free KDP   My Own

    ISBN _____

    Imprint _____

    Publication Date _____

Print Options circle one

    Black & white interior with cream paper

    Black & white interior with white paper

    Color interior with white paper

    Trim Size chosen: _____

Book Title _____

Bleed settings   No Bleed   Bleed

Paperback cover finish (circle one)   Matte   Glossy

Manuscript

     File name _____

     Uploaded   Date _____

     Updated   Date _____

     Updated   Date _____

     Updated   Date _____

     Interior Formatter _____

     Contact Info: _____

     Cost: _____

Book Cover

     File name _____

     Uploaded   Date _____

     Updated   Date _____

     Updated   Date _____

     Updated   Date _____

     Cover Designer _____

     Contact Info: _____

     Cost: _____

Book Preview - Approved Date _____

     Downloaded a PDF Proof   Date _____

Summary

     Page Count _____ Your Printing Cost _____

     Notes _____

     _____

Book Title _____

Paperback Rights & Pricing

Territories (circle one)

    All territories

    Individual territories

_____

_____

_____

_____

_____

Pricing & Royalty

    Primary Marketplace _____

    List Price Chosen _____ Currency ____

    Rate _____ Printing _____ Royalty _____

    Expanded Distribution?   Yes   No

    * Other Marketplace _____

    List Price Chosen _____ Currency ____

    Rate _____ Printing _____ Royalty _____

    * Other Marketplace _____

    List Price Chosen _____ Currency ____

    Rate _____ Printing _____ Royalty _____

    * Other Marketplace _____

    List Price Chosen _____ Currency ____

    Rate _____ Printing _____ Royalty _____

Book Title _____

* Other Marketplace _____

List Price Chosen _____ Currency ____

Rate _____ Printing _____ Royalty _____

* Other Marketplace _____

List Price Chosen _____ Currency ____

Rate _____ Printing _____ Royalty _____

* Other Marketplace _____

List Price Chosen _____ Currency ____

Rate _____ Printing _____ Royalty _____

Proof Copies

Requested a proof copy   Date _____

Arrival Date _____

Publication Status

Saved as Draft Date _____

Clicked Publish Button Date _____

Published Notice from KDP Date _____

Notes _____

_____

_____

_____

_____

_____

_____

_____

Book Title _____

Author Copy Orders

Date	#	Ship Speed	Ship Cost	Tax	Total	Arrived

Book Title _____

Note Date & Changes Made

_____

_____

_____

_____

_____

_____

_____

_____

_____

_____

_____

_____

_____

_____

_____

_____

_____

_____

_____

_____

_____

_____

_____

_____

_____

_____

Book Title _____

Note Date & Changes Made

_____
_____
_____
_____
_____
_____
_____
_____
_____
_____
_____
_____
_____
_____
_____
_____
_____
_____
_____
_____
_____
_____
_____
_____

BOOK 2 - Date _____

Paperback Details

Language _____

Book Title _____

Subtitle _____

Series _____ # _____

Edition Number (if it applies) _____

Author _____

Contributors (if any) _____

_____

_____

_____

Description: _____

_____

_____

_____

_____

_____

_____

_____

_____

_____

_____

_____

_____

Publishing Rights (circle or underline one)

I own the copyright

This is a public domain work

9

Book Title _____

Keywords (seven words or phrases)

_____

_____

_____

_____

_____

_____

_____

Categories (two)

_____

_____

_____

Large Print   No Yes

Adult Content   No Yes

Paperback Content

Print ISBN (circle one)   Free KDP   My Own

ISBN _____

Imprint _____

Publication Date _____

Print Options circle one

Black & white interior with cream paper

Black & white interior with white paper

Color interior with white paper

Trim Size chosen: _____

Book Title _____

Bleed settings   No Bleed   Bleed

Paperback cover finish (circle one)   Matte   Glossy

Manuscript

    File name _____

    Uploaded   Date _____

    Updated   Date _____

    Updated   Date _____

    Updated   Date _____

    Interior Formatter _____

    Contact Info: _____

    Cost: _____

Book Cover

    File name _____

    Uploaded   Date _____

    Updated   Date _____

    Updated   Date _____

    Updated   Date _____

    Cover Designer _____

    Contact Info: _____

    Cost: _____

Book Preview - Approved Date _____

    Downloaded a PDF Proof   Date _____

Summary

    Page Count _____ Your Printing Cost _____

    Notes _____

    _____

Book Title _____

Paperback Rights & Pricing

Territories (circle one)

    All territories

    Individual territories

_____

_____

_____

_____

_____

_____

Pricing & Royalty

    Primary Marketplace _____

    List Price Chosen _____ Currency ____

    Rate _____ Printing _____ Royalty _____

    Expanded Distribution?   Yes   No

    * Other Marketplace _____

    List Price Chosen _____ Currency ____

    Rate _____ Printing _____ Royalty _____

    * Other Marketplace _____

    List Price Chosen _____ Currency ____

    Rate _____ Printing _____ Royalty _____

    * Other Marketplace _____

    List Price Chosen _____ Currency ____

    Rate _____ Printing _____ Royalty _____

Book Title _____

* Other Marketplace _____

List Price Chosen _____ Currency _____

Rate _____ Printing _____ Royalty _____

* Other Marketplace _____

List Price Chosen _____ Currency _____

Rate _____ Printing _____ Royalty _____

* Other Marketplace _____

List Price Chosen _____ Currency _____

Rate _____ Printing _____ Royalty _____

Proof Copies

Requested a proof copy   Date _____

Arrival Date _____

Publication Status

Saved as Draft Date _____

Clicked Publish Button Date _____

Published Notice from KDP Date _____

Notes _____

_____

_____

_____

_____

_____

_____

_____

Book Title _____

Author Copy Orders

Date	#	Ship Speed	Ship Cost	Tax	Total	Arrived

Book Title _____

Note Date & Changes Made

_____

_____

_____

_____

_____

_____

_____

_____

_____

_____

_____

_____

_____

_____

_____

_____

_____

_____

_____

_____

_____

_____

Book Title _____

Note Date & Changes Made

_____
_____
_____
_____
_____
_____
_____
_____
_____
_____
_____
_____
_____
_____
_____
_____
_____
_____
_____
_____
_____
_____

BOOK 3 - Date _____

Paperback Details

Language _____

Book Title _____

Subtitle _____

Series _____ # _____

Edition Number (if it applies) _____

Author _____

Contributors (if any) _____

_____

_____

_____

Description: _____

_____

_____

_____

_____

_____

_____

_____

_____

_____

_____

_____

_____

Publishing Rights (circle or underline one)

I own the copyright

This is a public domain work

Book Title _____

Keywords (seven words or phrases)

_____

_____

_____

_____

_____

_____

_____

Categories (two)

_____

_____

_____

Large Print   No Yes

Adult Content   No Yes

Paperback Content

Print ISBN (circle one)   Free KDP   My Own

   ISBN _____

   Imprint _____

   Publication Date _____

Print Options circle one

   Black & white interior with cream paper

   Black & white interior with white paper

   Color interior with white paper

   Trim Size chosen: _____

Book Title _____

Bleed settings   No Bleed   Bleed

Paperback cover finish (circle one)   Matte   Glossy

Manuscript

File name _____

Uploaded   Date _____

Updated   Date _____

Updated   Date _____

Updated   Date _____

Interior Formatter _____

Contact Info: _____

Cost: _____

Book Cover

File name _____

Uploaded   Date _____

Updated   Date _____

Updated   Date _____

Updated   Date _____

Cover Designer _____

Contact Info: _____

Cost: _____

Book Preview - Approved Date _____

Downloaded a PDF Proof   Date _____

Summary

Page Count _____ Your Printing Cost _____

Notes _____

_____

Book Title _____

Paperback Rights & Pricing

Territories (circle one)

    All territories

    Individual territories

_____

_____

_____

_____

_____

_____

Pricing & Royalty

    Primary Marketplace _____

    List Price Chosen _____ Currency ____

    Rate _____ Printing _____ Royalty _____

    Expanded Distribution?   Yes   No

    * Other Marketplace _____

    List Price Chosen _____ Currency ____

    Rate _____ Printing _____ Royalty _____

    * Other Marketplace _____

    List Price Chosen _____ Currency ____

    Rate _____ Printing _____ Royalty _____

    * Other Marketplace _____

    List Price Chosen _____ Currency ____

    Rate _____ Printing _____ Royalty _____

Book Title _____

    * Other Marketplace _____

    List Price Chosen _____ Currency _____

    Rate _____ Printing _____ Royalty _____

    * Other Marketplace _____

    List Price Chosen _____ Currency _____

    Rate _____ Printing _____ Royalty _____

    * Other Marketplace _____

    List Price Chosen _____ Currency _____

    Rate _____ Printing _____ Royalty _____

Proof Copies

    Requested a proof copy   Date _____

    Arrival Date _____

Publication Status

    Saved as Draft Date _____

    Clicked Publish Button Date _____

    Published Notice from KDP Date _____

    Notes _____

    _____

    _____

    _____

    _____

    _____

    _____

    _____

Book Title _____

Author Copy Orders

Date	#	Ship Speed	Ship Cost	Tax	Total	Arrived

Book Title _____

Note Date & Changes Made

_____

_____

_____

_____

_____

_____

_____

_____

_____

_____

_____

_____

_____

_____

_____

_____

_____

_____

_____

_____

_____

_____

_____

_____

Book Title _____

Note Date & Changes Made

_____

_____

_____

_____

_____

_____

_____

_____

_____

_____

_____

_____

_____

_____

_____

_____

_____

_____

_____

_____

_____

_____

_____

_____

_____

BOOK 4 - Date _____

Paperback Details

Language _____

Book Title _____

Subtitle _____

Series _____ # ____

Edition Number (if it applies) _____

Author _____

Contributors (if any) _____

_____

_____

_____

Description: _____

_____

_____

_____

_____

_____

_____

_____

_____

_____

_____

_____

Publishing Rights (circle or underline one)

I own the copyright

This is a public domain work

25

Book Title _____

Keywords (seven words or phrases)

_____

_____

_____

_____

_____

_____

_____

Categories (two)

_____

_____

_____

Large Print   No Yes

Adult Content   No Yes

Paperback Content

Print ISBN (circle one)   Free KDP   My Own

   ISBN _____

   Imprint _____

   Publication Date _____

Print Options circle one

   Black & white interior with cream paper

   Black & white interior with white paper

   Color interior with white paper

   Trim Size chosen: _____

Book Title _____

Bleed settings   No Bleed   Bleed

Paperback cover finish (circle one)   Matte   Glossy

Manuscript

     File name _____

     Uploaded   Date _____

     Updated   Date _____

     Updated   Date _____

     Updated   Date _____

     Interior Formatter _____

     Contact Info: _____

     Cost: _____

Book Cover

     File name _____

     Uploaded   Date _____

     Updated   Date _____

     Updated   Date _____

     Updated   Date _____

     Cover Designer _____

     Contact Info: _____

     Cost: _____

Book Preview - Approved Date _____

     Downloaded a PDF Proof   Date _____

Summary

     Page Count _____ Your Printing Cost _____

     Notes _____

     _____

Book Title _____

Paperback Rights & Pricing

Territories (circle one)

    All territories

    Individual territories

_____

_____

_____

_____

_____

_____

Pricing & Royalty

    Primary Marketplace _____

    List Price Chosen _____ Currency _____

    Rate _____ Printing _____ Royalty _____

    Expanded Distribution?   Yes   No

    * Other Marketplace _____

    List Price Chosen _____ Currency _____

    Rate _____ Printing _____ Royalty _____

    * Other Marketplace _____

    List Price Chosen _____ Currency _____

    Rate _____ Printing _____ Royalty _____

    * Other Marketplace _____

    List Price Chosen _____ Currency _____

    Rate _____ Printing _____ Royalty _____

Book Title _____

    * Other Marketplace _____

    List Price Chosen _____ Currency _____

    Rate _____ Printing _____ Royalty _____

    * Other Marketplace _____

    List Price Chosen _____ Currency _____

    Rate _____ Printing _____ Royalty _____

    * Other Marketplace _____

    List Price Chosen _____ Currency _____

    Rate _____ Printing _____ Royalty _____

Proof Copies

    Requested a proof copy   Date _____

    Arrival Date _____

Publication Status

    Saved as Draft Date _____

    Clicked Publish Button Date _____

    Published Notice from KDP Date _____

    Notes _____

    _____

    _____

    _____

    _____

    _____

    _____

    _____

Book Title _____

Author Copy Orders

Date	#	Ship Speed	Ship Cost	Tax	Total	Arrived

Book Title _____

Note Date & Changes Made

_____

_____

_____

_____

_____

_____

_____

_____

_____

_____

_____

_____

_____

_____

_____

_____

_____

_____

_____

_____

_____

_____

Book Title _____

Note Date & Changes Made

_____

_____

_____

_____

_____

_____

_____

_____

_____

_____

_____

_____

_____

_____

_____

_____

_____

_____

_____

_____

_____

_____

_____

_____

_____

BOOK 5 - Date _____

Paperback Details

Language _____

Book Title _____

Subtitle _____

Series _____ # ____

Edition Number (if it applies) _____

Author _____

Contributors (if any) _____

_____

_____

_____

Description: _____

_____

_____

_____

_____

_____

_____

_____

_____

_____

_____

_____

_____

Publishing Rights (circle or underline one)

        I own the copyright

        This is a public domain work

Book Title _____

Keywords (seven words or phrases)

_____

_____

_____

_____

_____

_____

_____

Categories (two)

_____

_____

_____

Large Print   No Yes

Adult Content   No Yes

Paperback Content

Print ISBN (circle one)   Free KDP   My Own

ISBN _____

Imprint _____

Publication Date _____

Print Options circle one

Black & white interior with cream paper

Black & white interior with white paper

Color interior with white paper

Trim Size chosen: _____

Book Title _____

    Bleed settings   No Bleed Bleed

    Paperback cover finish (circle one)   Matte   Glossy

Manuscript

    File name _____

    Uploaded   Date _____

    Updated   Date _____

    Updated   Date _____

    Updated   Date _____

    Interior Formatter _____

    Contact Info: _____

    Cost: _____

Book Cover

    File name _____

    Uploaded   Date _____

    Updated   Date _____

    Updated   Date _____

    Updated   Date _____

    Cover Designer _____

    Contact Info: _____

    Cost: _____

Book Preview - Approved Date _____

    Downloaded a PDF Proof   Date _____

Summary

    Page Count _____ Your Printing Cost _____

    Notes _____

    _____

Book Title _____

Paperback Rights & Pricing

Territories (circle one)

    All territories

    Individual territories

_____

_____

_____

_____

_____

_____

Pricing & Royalty

    Primary Marketplace _____

    List Price Chosen _____ Currency _____

    Rate _____ Printing _____ Royalty _____

    Expanded Distribution?   Yes   No

    * Other Marketplace _____

    List Price Chosen _____ Currency _____

    Rate _____ Printing _____ Royalty _____

    * Other Marketplace _____

    List Price Chosen _____ Currency _____

    Rate _____ Printing _____ Royalty _____

    * Other Marketplace _____

    List Price Chosen _____ Currency _____

    Rate _____ Printing _____ Royalty _____

Book Title _____

* Other Marketplace _____

List Price Chosen _____ Currency ____

Rate _____ Printing _____ Royalty _____

* Other Marketplace _____

List Price Chosen _____ Currency ____

Rate _____ Printing _____ Royalty _____

* Other Marketplace _____

List Price Chosen _____ Currency ____

Rate _____ Printing _____ Royalty _____

Proof Copies

Requested a proof copy   Date _____

Arrival Date _____

Publication Status

Saved as Draft Date _____

Clicked Publish Button Date _____

Published Notice from KDP Date _____

Notes _____

_____

_____

_____

_____

_____

_____

_____

Book Title _____

Author Copy Orders

Date	#	Ship Speed	Ship Cost	Tax	Total	Arrived

Book Title _____

Note Date & Changes Made

_____

_____

_____

_____

_____

_____

_____

_____

_____

_____

_____

_____

_____

_____

_____

_____

_____

_____

_____

_____

_____

_____

_____

Book Title _____

Note Date & Changes Made

_____

_____

_____

_____

_____

_____

_____

_____

_____

_____

_____

_____

_____

_____

_____

_____

_____

_____

_____

_____

_____

_____

BOOK 6 - Date _____

Paperback Details

Language _____

Book Title _____

Subtitle _____

Series _____ # ____

Edition Number (if it applies) _____

Author _____

Contributors (if any) _____

_____

_____

_____

Description: _____

_____

_____

_____

_____

_____

_____

_____

_____

_____

_____

_____

_____

Publishing Rights (circle or underline one)

I own the copyright

This is a public domain work

Book Title _____

Keywords (seven words or phrases)

_____

_____

_____

_____

_____

_____

_____

Categories (two)

_____

_____

_____

Large Print   No Yes

Adult Content   No Yes

Paperback Content

Print ISBN (circle one)   **Free KDP**   **My Own**

ISBN _____

Imprint _____

Publication Date _____

Print Options circle one

Black & white interior with cream paper

Black & white interior with white paper

Color interior with white paper

Trim Size chosen: _____

Book Title _____

    Bleed settings   No Bleed   Bleed

    Paperback cover finish (circle one)   Matte   Glossy

Manuscript

    File name _____

    Uploaded   Date _____

    Updated   Date _____

    Updated   Date _____

    Updated   Date _____

    Interior Formatter _____

    Contact Info: _____

    Cost: _____

Book Cover

    File name _____

    Uploaded   Date _____

    Updated   Date _____

    Updated   Date _____

    Updated   Date _____

    Cover Designer _____

    Contact Info: _____

    Cost: _____

Book Preview - Approved Date _____

    Downloaded a PDF Proof   Date _____

Summary

    Page Count _____ Your Printing Cost _____

    Notes _____

    _____

Book Title _____

Paperback Rights & Pricing

Territories (circle one)

    All territories

    Individual territories

_____

_____

_____

_____

_____

_____

Pricing & Royalty

    Primary Marketplace _____

    List Price Chosen _____ Currency ____

    Rate _____ Printing _____ Royalty _____

    Expanded Distribution?   Yes   No

    * Other Marketplace _____

    List Price Chosen _____ Currency ____

    Rate _____ Printing _____ Royalty _____

    * Other Marketplace _____

    List Price Chosen _____ Currency ____

    Rate _____ Printing _____ Royalty _____

    * Other Marketplace _____

    List Price Chosen _____ Currency ____

    Rate _____ Printing _____ Royalty _____

Book Title _____

    * Other Marketplace _____

    List Price Chosen _____ Currency ____

    Rate _____ Printing _____ Royalty _____

    * Other Marketplace _____

    List Price Chosen _____ Currency ____

    Rate _____ Printing _____ Royalty _____

    * Other Marketplace _____

    List Price Chosen _____ Currency ____

    Rate _____ Printing _____ Royalty _____

Proof Copies

    Requested a proof copy   Date _____

    Arrival Date _____

Publication Status

    Saved as Draft Date _____

    Clicked Publish Button Date _____

    Published Notice from KDP Date _____

    Notes _____

    _____

    _____

    _____

    _____

    _____

    _____

    _____

Book Title _____

Author Copy Orders

Date   # Ship Speed Ship Cost Tax Total Arrived

_____

_____

_____

_____

_____

_____

_____

_____

_____

_____

_____

_____

_____

_____

_____

_____

_____

_____

_____

_____

_____

_____

Book Title _____

Note Date & Changes Made

_____

_____

_____

_____

_____

_____

_____

_____

_____

_____

_____

_____

_____

_____

_____

_____

_____

_____

_____

_____

_____

_____

_____

_____

_____

_____

Book Title _____

Note Date & Changes Made

_____
_____
_____
_____
_____
_____
_____
_____
_____
_____
_____
_____
_____
_____
_____
_____
_____
_____
_____
_____
_____
_____
_____

BOOK 7 - Date _____

Paperback Details

Language _____

Book Title _____

Subtitle _____

Series _____ # _____

Edition Number (if it applies) _____

Author _____

Contributors (if any) _____

_____

_____

_____

Description: _____

_____

_____

_____

_____

_____

_____

_____

_____

_____

_____

_____

_____

Publishing Rights (circle or underline one)

I own the copyright

This is a public domain work

Book Title _____

Keywords (seven words or phrases)

_____

_____

_____

_____

_____

_____

_____

Categories (two)

_____

_____

_____

Large Print   No Yes

Adult Content   No Yes

Paperback Content

Print ISBN (circle one)   Free KDP   My Own

ISBN _____

Imprint _____

Publication Date _____

Print Options circle one

Black & white interior with cream paper

Black & white interior with white paper

Color interior with white paper

Trim Size chosen: _____

Book Title _____

Bleed settings   No Bleed   Bleed

Paperback cover finish (circle one)   Matte   Glossy

Manuscript

    File name _____

    Uploaded   Date _____

    Updated   Date _____

    Updated   Date _____

    Updated   Date _____

    Interior Formatter _____

    Contact Info: _____

    Cost: _____

Book Cover

    File name _____

    Uploaded   Date _____

    Updated   Date _____

    Updated   Date _____

    Updated   Date _____

    Cover Designer _____

    Contact Info: _____

    Cost: _____

Book Preview - Approved Date _____

    Downloaded a PDF Proof   Date _____

Summary

    Page Count _____ Your Printing Cost _____

    Notes _____

    _____

Book Title _____

Paperback Rights & Pricing

Territories (circle one)

    All territories

    Individual territories

_____

_____

_____

_____

_____

_____

Pricing & Royalty

    Primary Marketplace _____

    List Price Chosen _____ Currency _____

    Rate _____ Printing _____ Royalty _____

    Expanded Distribution?   Yes   No

    * Other Marketplace _____

    List Price Chosen _____ Currency _____

    Rate _____ Printing _____ Royalty _____

    * Other Marketplace _____

    List Price Chosen _____ Currency _____

    Rate _____ Printing _____ Royalty _____

    * Other Marketplace _____

    List Price Chosen _____ Currency _____

    Rate _____ Printing _____ Royalty _____

Book Title _____

* Other Marketplace _____

List Price Chosen _____ Currency _____

Rate _____ Printing _____ Royalty _____

* Other Marketplace _____

List Price Chosen _____ Currency _____

Rate _____ Printing _____ Royalty _____

* Other Marketplace _____

List Price Chosen _____ Currency _____

Rate _____ Printing _____ Royalty _____

Proof Copies

Requested a proof copy   Date _____

Arrival Date _____

Publication Status

Saved as Draft Date _____

Clicked Publish Button Date _____

Published Notice from KDP Date _____

Notes _____

_____

_____

_____

_____

_____

_____

Book Title _____

Author Copy Orders

Date	#	Ship Speed	Ship Cost	Tax	Total	Arrived

Book Title _____

Note Date & Changes Made

_____

_____

_____

_____

_____

_____

_____

_____

_____

_____

_____

_____

_____

_____

_____

_____

_____

_____

_____

_____

_____

_____

_____

Book Title _____

Note Date & Changes Made

BOOK 8 - Date _____

Paperback Details

Language _____

Book Title _____

Subtitle _____

Series _____ # ____

Edition Number (if it applies) _____

Author _____

Contributors (if any) _____

_____

_____

_____

Description: _____

_____

_____

_____

_____

_____

_____

_____

_____

_____

_____

_____

_____

Publishing Rights (circle or underline one)

I own the copyright

This is a public domain work

Book Title _____

Keywords (seven words or phrases)

_____

_____

_____

_____

_____

_____

_____

Categories (two)

_____

_____

_____

Large Print   No Yes

Adult Content   No Yes

Paperback Content

Print ISBN (circle one)   Free KDP   My Own

    ISBN _____

    Imprint _____

    Publication Date _____

Print Options circle one

    Black & white interior with cream paper

    Black & white interior with white paper

    Color interior with white paper

    Trim Size chosen: _____

Book Title _____

Bleed settings   No Bleed   Bleed

Paperback cover finish (circle one)   Matte   Glossy

Manuscript

File name _____

Uploaded   Date _____

Updated   Date _____

Updated   Date _____

Updated   Date _____

Interior Formatter _____

Contact Info: _____

Cost: _____

Book Cover

File name _____

Uploaded   Date _____

Updated   Date _____

Updated   Date _____

Updated   Date _____

Cover Designer _____

Contact Info: _____

Cost: _____

Book Preview - Approved Date _____

Downloaded a PDF Proof   Date _____

Summary

Page Count _____ Your Printing Cost _____

Notes _____

_____

Book Title _____

Paperback Rights & Pricing

Territories (circle one)

    All territories

    Individual territories

_____

_____

_____

_____

_____

_____

Pricing & Royalty

    Primary Marketplace _____

    List Price Chosen _____ Currency _____

    Rate _____ Printing _____ Royalty _____

    Expanded Distribution?   Yes   No

    * Other Marketplace _____

    List Price Chosen _____ Currency _____

    Rate _____ Printing _____ Royalty _____

    * Other Marketplace _____

    List Price Chosen _____ Currency _____

    Rate _____ Printing _____ Royalty _____

    * Other Marketplace _____

    List Price Chosen _____ Currency _____

    Rate _____ Printing _____ Royalty _____

Book Title _____

* Other Marketplace _____

List Price Chosen _____ Currency _____

Rate _____ Printing _____ Royalty _____

* Other Marketplace _____

List Price Chosen _____ Currency _____

Rate _____ Printing _____ Royalty _____

* Other Marketplace _____

List Price Chosen _____ Currency _____

Rate _____ Printing _____ Royalty _____

Proof Copies

Requested a proof copy   Date _____

Arrival Date _____

Publication Status

Saved as Draft Date _____

Clicked Publish Button Date _____

Published Notice from KDP Date _____

Notes _____

_____

_____

_____

_____

_____

_____

_____

Book Title _____

Author Copy Orders

Date	#	Ship Speed	Ship Cost	Tax	Total	Arrived

Book Title _____

Note Date & Changes Made

_____

_____

_____

_____

_____

_____

_____

_____

_____

_____

_____

_____

_____

_____

_____

_____

_____

_____

_____

_____

_____

_____

_____

Book Title _____

Note Date & Changes Made

_____

_____

_____

_____

_____

_____

_____

_____

_____

_____

_____

_____

_____

_____

_____

_____

_____

_____

_____

_____

_____

_____

BOOK 9 - Date _____

Paperback Details

Language _____

Book Title _____

Subtitle _____

Series _____ # _____

Edition Number (if it applies) _____

Author _____

Contributors (if any) _____

_____

_____

_____

Description: _____

_____

_____

_____

_____

_____

_____

_____

_____

_____

_____

_____

Publishing Rights (circle or underline one)

I own the copyright

This is a public domain work

Book Title _____

Keywords (seven words or phrases)

_____

_____

_____

_____

_____

_____

_____

Categories (two)

_____

_____

_____

Large Print   No Yes

Adult Content   No Yes

Paperback Content

Print ISBN (circle one)   Free KDP   My Own

   ISBN _____

   Imprint _____

   Publication Date _____

Print Options circle one

   Black & white interior with cream paper

   Black & white interior with white paper

   Color interior with white paper

   Trim Size chosen: _____

Book Title _____

    Bleed settings   No Bleed   Bleed

    Paperback cover finish (circle one)   Matte   Glossy

Manuscript

    File name _____

    Uploaded   Date _____

    Updated   Date _____

    Updated   Date _____

    Updated   Date _____

    Interior Formatter _____

    Contact Info: _____

    Cost: _____

Book Cover

    File name _____

    Uploaded   Date _____

    Updated   Date _____

    Updated   Date _____

    Updated   Date _____

    Cover Designer _____

    Contact Info: _____

    Cost: _____

Book Preview - Approved Date _____

    Downloaded a PDF Proof   Date _____

Summary

    Page Count _____ Your Printing Cost _____

    Notes _____

    _____

Book Title _____

Paperback Rights & Pricing

Territories (circle one)

    All territories

    Individual territories

_____

_____

_____

_____

_____

_____

Pricing & Royalty

    Primary Marketplace _____

    List Price Chosen _____ Currency ____

    Rate _____ Printing _____ Royalty _____

    Expanded Distribution?   Yes   No

    * Other Marketplace _____

    List Price Chosen _____ Currency ____

    Rate _____ Printing _____ Royalty _____

    * Other Marketplace _____

    List Price Chosen _____ Currency ____

    Rate _____ Printing _____ Royalty _____

    * Other Marketplace _____

    List Price Chosen _____ Currency ____

    Rate _____ Printing _____ Royalty _____

Book Title _____

* Other Marketplace _____

List Price Chosen _____ Currency ____

Rate _____ Printing _____ Royalty _____

* Other Marketplace _____

List Price Chosen _____ Currency ____

Rate _____ Printing _____ Royalty _____

* Other Marketplace _____

List Price Chosen _____ Currency ____

Rate _____ Printing _____ Royalty _____

Proof Copies

Requested a proof copy   Date _____

Arrival Date _____

Publication Status

Saved as Draft Date _____

Clicked Publish Button Date _____

Published Notice from KDP Date _____

Notes _____

_____

_____

_____

_____

_____

_____

_____

Book Title _____

Author Copy Orders

Date	#	Ship Speed	Ship Cost	Tax	Total	Arrived

Book Title _____

Note Date & Changes Made

_____

_____

_____

_____

_____

_____

_____

_____

_____

_____

_____

_____

_____

_____

_____

_____

_____

_____

_____

_____

_____

_____

Book Title _____

Note Date & Changes Made

_____

_____

_____

_____

_____

_____

_____

_____

_____

_____

_____

_____

_____

_____

_____

_____

_____

_____

_____

_____

_____

BOOK 10 - Date _____

Paperback Details

Language _____

Book Title _____

Subtitle _____

Series _____ # ____

Edition Number (if it applies) _____

Author _____

Contributors (if any) _____

_____

_____

_____

Description: _____

_____

_____

_____

_____

_____

_____

_____

_____

_____

_____

_____

_____

Publishing Rights (circle or underline one)

I own the copyright

This is a public domain work

Book Title _____

Keywords (seven words or phrases)

_____

_____

_____

_____

_____

_____

_____

Categories (two)

_____

_____

_____

Large Print   No Yes

Adult Content   No Yes

Paperback Content

Print ISBN (circle one)   Free KDP   My Own

ISBN _____

Imprint _____

Publication Date _____

Print Options circle one

Black & white interior with cream paper

Black & white interior with white paper

Color interior with white paper

Trim Size chosen: _____

Book Title _____

Bleed settings   No Bleed   Bleed

Paperback cover finish (circle one)   Matte   Glossy

Manuscript

File name _____

Uploaded   Date _____

Updated   Date _____

Updated   Date _____

Updated   Date _____

Interior Formatter _____

Contact Info: _____

Cost: _____

Book Cover

File name _____

Uploaded   Date _____

Updated   Date _____

Updated   Date _____

Updated   Date _____

Cover Designer _____

Contact Info: _____

Cost: _____

Book Preview - Approved Date _____

Downloaded a PDF Proof   Date _____

Summary

Page Count _____ Your Printing Cost _____

Notes _____

_____

Book Title _____

Paperback Rights & Pricing

Territories (circle one)

    All territories

    Individual territories

_____

_____

_____

_____

_____

_____

Pricing & Royalty

    Primary Marketplace _____

    List Price Chosen _____ Currency ____

    Rate _____ Printing _____ Royalty _____

    Expanded Distribution?   Yes   No

    * Other Marketplace _____

    List Price Chosen _____ Currency ____

    Rate _____ Printing _____ Royalty _____

    * Other Marketplace _____

    List Price Chosen _____ Currency ____

    Rate _____ Printing _____ Royalty _____

    * Other Marketplace _____

    List Price Chosen _____ Currency ____

    Rate _____ Printing _____ Royalty _____

Book Title _____

* Other Marketplace _____

List Price Chosen _____ Currency _____

Rate _____ Printing _____ Royalty _____

* Other Marketplace _____

List Price Chosen _____ Currency _____

Rate _____ Printing _____ Royalty _____

* Other Marketplace _____

List Price Chosen _____ Currency _____

Rate _____ Printing _____ Royalty _____

Proof Copies

Requested a proof copy   Date _____

Arrival Date _____

Publication Status

Saved as Draft Date _____

Clicked Publish Button Date _____

Published Notice from KDP Date _____

Notes _____

_____

_____

_____

_____

_____

_____

_____

Book Title _____

Author Copy Orders

Date	#	Ship Speed	Ship Cost	Tax	Total	Arrived

Book Title _____

Note Date & Changes Made

_____

_____

_____

_____

_____

_____

_____

_____

_____

_____

_____

_____

_____

_____

_____

_____

_____

_____

_____

_____

_____

Book Title _____

Note Date & Changes Made

_____
_____
_____
_____
_____
_____
_____
_____
_____
_____
_____
_____
_____
_____
_____
_____
_____
_____
_____
_____
_____
_____
_____
_____
_____

BOOK 11 - Date _____

Paperback Details

Language _____

Book Title _____

Subtitle _____

Series _____ # _____

Edition Number (if it applies) _____

Author _____

Contributors (if any) _____

_____

_____

_____

Description: _____

_____

_____

_____

_____

_____

_____

_____

_____

_____

_____

_____

_____

Publishing Rights (circle or underline one)

I own the copyright

This is a public domain work

Book Title _____

    Keywords (seven words or phrases)

_____

_____

_____

_____

_____

_____

_____

    Categories (two)

_____

_____

_____

_____

Large Print   No Yes

Adult Content   No Yes

Paperback Content

Print ISBN (circle one)   Free KDP   My Own

    ISBN _____

    Imprint _____

    Publication Date _____

Print Options circle one

    Black & white interior with cream paper

    Black & white interior with white paper

    Color interior with white paper

    Trim Size chosen: _____

Book Title _____

    Bleed settings   No Bleed   Bleed

    Paperback cover finish (circle one)   Matte   Glossy

Manuscript

    File name _____

    Uploaded   Date _____

    Updated   Date _____

    Updated   Date _____

    Updated   Date _____

    Interior Formatter _____

    Contact Info: _____

    Cost: _____

Book Cover

    File name _____

    Uploaded   Date _____

    Updated   Date _____

    Updated   Date _____

    Updated   Date _____

    Cover Designer _____

    Contact Info: _____

    Cost: _____

Book Preview - Approved Date _____

    Downloaded a PDF Proof   Date _____

Summary

    Page Count _____ Your Printing Cost _____

    Notes _____

    _____

Book Title _____

Paperback Rights & Pricing

Territories (circle one)

    All territories

    Individual territories

_____

_____

_____

_____

_____

_____

Pricing & Royalty

    Primary Marketplace _____

    List Price Chosen _____ Currency _____

    Rate _____ Printing _____ Royalty _____

    Expanded Distribution?   Yes   No

    * Other Marketplace _____

    List Price Chosen _____ Currency _____

    Rate _____ Printing _____ Royalty _____

    * Other Marketplace _____

    List Price Chosen _____ Currency _____

    Rate _____ Printing _____ Royalty _____

    * Other Marketplace _____

    List Price Chosen _____ Currency _____

    Rate _____ Printing _____ Royalty _____

Book Title _____

* Other Marketplace _____

List Price Chosen _____ Currency _____

Rate _____ Printing _____ Royalty _____

* Other Marketplace _____

List Price Chosen _____ Currency _____

Rate _____ Printing _____ Royalty _____

* Other Marketplace _____

List Price Chosen _____ Currency _____

Rate _____ Printing _____ Royalty _____

Proof Copies

Requested a proof copy   Date _____

Arrival Date _____

Publication Status

Saved as Draft Date _____

Clicked Publish Button Date _____

Published Notice from KDP Date _____

Notes _____

_____

_____

_____

_____

_____

_____

_____

Book Title _____

Author Copy Orders

Date	#	Ship Speed	Ship Cost	Tax	Total	Arrived

Book Title _____

Note Date & Changes Made

_____

_____

_____

_____

_____

_____

_____

_____

_____

_____

_____

_____

_____

_____

_____

_____

_____

_____

_____

_____

_____

_____

_____

Book Title _____

Note Date & Changes Made

_____

_____

_____

_____

_____

_____

_____

_____

_____

_____

_____

_____

_____

_____

_____

_____

_____

_____

_____

_____

_____

_____

BOOK 12 - Date _____

Paperback Details

Language _____

Book Title _____

Subtitle _____

Series _____ # _____

Edition Number (if it applies) _____

Author _____

Contributors (if any) _____

_____

_____

_____

Description: _____

_____

_____

_____

_____

_____

_____

_____

_____

_____

_____

_____

_____

Publishing Rights (circle or underline one)

I own the copyright

This is a public domain work

Book Title _____

Keywords (seven words or phrases)

_____

_____

_____

_____

_____

_____

_____

Categories (two)

_____

_____

_____

| Large Print | No Yes |
| Adult Content | No Yes |

Paperback Content

Print ISBN (circle one)   Free KDP   My Own

   ISBN _____

   Imprint _____

   Publication Date _____

Print Options circle one

   Black & white interior with cream paper

   Black & white interior with white paper

   Color interior with white paper

   Trim Size chosen: _____

Book Title _____

    Bleed settings   No Bleed Bleed

    Paperback cover finish (circle one)   Matte   Glossy

Manuscript

    File name _____

    Uploaded   Date _____

    Updated   Date _____

    Updated   Date _____

    Updated   Date _____

    Interior Formatter _____

    Contact Info: _____

    Cost: _____

Book Cover

    File name _____

    Uploaded   Date _____

    Updated   Date _____

    Updated   Date _____

    Updated   Date _____

    Cover Designer _____

    Contact Info: _____

    Cost: _____

Book Preview - Approved Date _____

    Downloaded a PDF Proof   Date _____

Summary

    Page Count _____ Your Printing Cost _____

    Notes _____

    _____

Book Title _____

Paperback Rights & Pricing

Territories (circle one)

    All territories

    Individual territories

_____

_____

_____

_____

_____

_____

Pricing & Royalty

    Primary Marketplace _____

    List Price Chosen _____ Currency ____

    Rate _____ Printing _____ Royalty _____

    Expanded Distribution?   Yes   No

    * Other Marketplace _____

    List Price Chosen _____ Currency ____

    Rate _____ Printing _____ Royalty _____

    * Other Marketplace _____

    List Price Chosen _____ Currency ____

    Rate _____ Printing _____ Royalty _____

    * Other Marketplace _____

    List Price Chosen _____ Currency ____

    Rate _____ Printing _____ Royalty _____

Book Title _____

* Other Marketplace _____

List Price Chosen _____ Currency ____

Rate _____ Printing _____ Royalty _____

* Other Marketplace _____

List Price Chosen _____ Currency ____

Rate _____ Printing _____ Royalty _____

* Other Marketplace _____

List Price Chosen _____ Currency ____

Rate _____ Printing _____ Royalty _____

Proof Copies

Requested a proof copy   Date _____

Arrival Date _____

Publication Status

Saved as Draft Date _____

Clicked Publish Button Date _____

Published Notice from KDP Date _____

Notes _____

_____

_____

_____

_____

_____

_____

_____

Book Title _____

Author Copy Orders

Date	#	Ship Speed	Ship Cost	Tax	Total	Arrived

Book Title _____

Note Date & Changes Made

_____

_____

_____

_____

_____

_____

_____

_____

_____

_____

_____

_____

_____

_____

_____

_____

_____

_____

_____

_____

_____

_____

_____

_____

_____

_____

Book Title _____

Note Date & Changes Made

BOOK 13 - Date _____

Paperback Details

Language _____

Book Title _____

Subtitle _____

Series _____ # ____

Edition Number (if it applies) _____

Author _____

Contributors (if any) _____

_____

_____

_____

Description: _____

_____

_____

_____

_____

_____

_____

_____

_____

_____

_____

_____

_____

Publishing Rights (circle or underline one)

      I own the copyright

      This is a public domain work

Book Title _____

Keywords (seven words or phrases)

_____

_____

_____

_____

_____

_____

_____

Categories (two)

_____

_____

_____

Large Print   No Yes

Adult Content   No Yes

Paperback Content

Print ISBN (circle one)   Free KDP   My Own

   ISBN _____

   Imprint _____

   Publication Date _____

Print Options circle one

   Black & white interior with cream paper

   Black & white interior with white paper

   Color interior with white paper

   Trim Size chosen: _____

Book Title _____

Bleed settings   No Bleed   Bleed

Paperback cover finish (circle one)   Matte   Glossy

Manuscript

     File name _____

     Uploaded   Date _____

     Updated   Date _____

     Updated   Date _____

     Updated   Date _____

     Interior Formatter _____

     Contact Info: _____

     Cost: _____

Book Cover

     File name _____

     Uploaded   Date _____

     Updated   Date _____

     Updated   Date _____

     Updated   Date _____

     Cover Designer _____

     Contact Info: _____

     Cost: _____

Book Preview - Approved Date _____

     Downloaded a PDF Proof   Date _____

Summary

     Page Count _____ Your Printing Cost _____

     Notes _____

     _____

Book Title _____

Paperback Rights & Pricing

Territories (circle one)

    All territories

    Individual territories

_____

_____

_____

_____

_____

_____

Pricing & Royalty

    Primary Marketplace _____

    List Price Chosen _____ Currency _____

    Rate _____ Printing _____ Royalty _____

    Expanded Distribution?   Yes   No

    * Other Marketplace _____

    List Price Chosen _____ Currency _____

    Rate _____ Printing _____ Royalty _____

    * Other Marketplace _____

    List Price Chosen _____ Currency _____

    Rate _____ Printing _____ Royalty _____

    * Other Marketplace _____

    List Price Chosen _____ Currency _____

    Rate _____ Printing _____ Royalty _____

Book Title _____

* Other Marketplace _____

List Price Chosen _____ Currency _____

Rate _____ Printing _____ Royalty _____

* Other Marketplace _____

List Price Chosen _____ Currency _____

Rate _____ Printing _____ Royalty _____

* Other Marketplace _____

List Price Chosen _____ Currency _____

Rate _____ Printing _____ Royalty _____

Proof Copies

Requested a proof copy   Date _____

Arrival Date _____

Publication Status

Saved as Draft Date _____

Clicked Publish Button Date _____

Published Notice from KDP Date _____

Notes _____

_____

_____

_____

_____

_____

_____

_____

Book Title _____

Author Copy Orders

Date   # Ship Speed Ship Cost Tax Total Arrived

_____

_____

_____

_____

_____

_____

_____

_____

_____

_____

_____

_____

_____

_____

_____

_____

_____

_____

_____

_____

_____

_____

_____

Book Title _____

Note Date & Changes Made

_____

_____

_____

_____

_____

_____

_____

_____

_____

_____

_____

_____

_____

_____

_____

_____

_____

_____

_____

_____

_____

_____

_____

Book Title _____

Note Date & Changes Made

_____

_____

_____

_____

_____

_____

_____

_____

_____

_____

_____

_____

_____

_____

_____

_____

_____

_____

_____

_____

_____

_____

_____

_____

_____

BOOK 14 - Date _____

Paperback Details

Language _____

Book Title _____

Subtitle _____

Series _____ # _____

Edition Number (if it applies) _____

Author _____

Contributors (if any) _____

_____

_____

_____

Description: _____

_____

_____

_____

_____

_____

_____

_____

_____

_____

_____

_____

_____

Publishing Rights (circle or underline one)

I own the copyright

This is a public domain work

Book Title _____

Keywords (seven words or phrases)

_____

_____

_____

_____

_____

_____

_____

Categories (two)

_____

_____

_____

Large Print   No Yes

Adult Content   No Yes

Paperback Content

Print ISBN (circle one)   Free KDP   My Own

ISBN _____

Imprint _____

Publication Date _____

Print Options circle one

Black & white interior with cream paper

Black & white interior with white paper

Color interior with white paper

Trim Size chosen: _____

Book Title _____

    Bleed settings   No Bleed   Bleed

    Paperback cover finish (circle one)   Matte   Glossy

Manuscript

    File name _____

    Uploaded   Date _____

    Updated   Date _____

    Updated   Date _____

    Updated   Date _____

    Interior Formatter _____

    Contact Info: _____

    Cost: _____

Book Cover

    File name _____

    Uploaded   Date _____

    Updated   Date _____

    Updated   Date _____

    Updated   Date _____

    Cover Designer _____

    Contact Info: _____

    Cost: _____

Book Preview - Approved Date _____

    Downloaded a PDF Proof   Date _____

Summary

    Page Count _____ Your Printing Cost _____

    Notes _____

    _____

Book Title _____

Paperback Rights & Pricing

Territories (circle one)

    All territories

    Individual territories

_____

_____

_____

_____

_____

_____

Pricing & Royalty

    Primary Marketplace _____

    List Price Chosen _____ Currency ____

    Rate _____ Printing _____ Royalty _____

    Expanded Distribution?   Yes   No

    * Other Marketplace _____

    List Price Chosen _____ Currency ____

    Rate _____ Printing _____ Royalty _____

    * Other Marketplace _____

    List Price Chosen _____ Currency ____

    Rate _____ Printing _____ Royalty _____

    * Other Marketplace _____

    List Price Chosen _____ Currency ____

    Rate _____ Printing _____ Royalty _____

Book Title _____

* Other Marketplace _____

List Price Chosen _____ Currency ____

Rate _____ Printing _____ Royalty _____

* Other Marketplace _____

List Price Chosen _____ Currency ____

Rate _____ Printing _____ Royalty _____

* Other Marketplace _____

List Price Chosen _____ Currency ____

Rate _____ Printing _____ Royalty _____

Proof Copies

Requested a proof copy   Date _____

Arrival Date _____

Publication Status

Saved as Draft Date _____

Clicked Publish Button Date _____

Published Notice from KDP Date _____

Notes _____

_____

_____

_____

_____

_____

_____

_____

Book Title _____

Author Copy Orders

Date   # Ship Speed Ship Cost Tax Total Arrived

_____

_____

_____

_____

_____

_____

_____

_____

_____

_____

_____

_____

_____

_____

_____

_____

_____

_____

_____

_____

_____

_____

Book Title _____

Note Date & Changes Made

_____

_____

_____

_____

_____

_____

_____

_____

_____

_____

_____

_____

_____

_____

_____

_____

_____

_____

_____

_____

_____

_____

_____

Book Title _____

Note Date & Changes Made

_____
_____
_____
_____
_____
_____
_____
_____
_____
_____
_____
_____
_____
_____
_____
_____
_____
_____
_____
_____
_____
_____
_____

BOOK 15 - Date _____

Paperback Details

Language _____

Book Title _____

Subtitle _____

Series _____ # _____

Edition Number (if it applies) _____

Author _____

Contributors (if any) _____

_____

_____

_____

Description: _____

_____

_____

_____

_____

_____

_____

_____

_____

_____

_____

_____

Publishing Rights (circle or underline one)

        I own the copyright

        This is a public domain work

Book Title _____

Keywords (seven words or phrases)

_____

_____

_____

_____

_____

_____

_____

Categories (two)

_____

_____

_____

Large Print   No Yes

Adult Content   No Yes

Paperback Content

Print ISBN (circle one)   Free KDP   My Own

     ISBN _____

     Imprint _____

     Publication Date _____

Print Options circle one

     Black & white interior with cream paper

     Black & white interior with white paper

     Color interior with white paper

     Trim Size chosen: _____

Book Title _____

    Bleed settings   No Bleed   Bleed

    Paperback cover finish (circle one)   Matte   Glossy

Manuscript

    File name _____

    Uploaded   Date _____

    Updated   Date _____

    Updated   Date _____

    Updated   Date _____

    Interior Formatter _____

    Contact Info: _____

    Cost: _____

Book Cover

    File name _____

    Uploaded   Date _____

    Updated   Date _____

    Updated   Date _____

    Updated   Date _____

    Cover Designer _____

    Contact Info: _____

    Cost: _____

Book Preview - Approved Date _____

    Downloaded a PDF Proof   Date _____

Summary

    Page Count _____ Your Printing Cost _____

    Notes _____

    _____

Book Title _____

Paperback Rights & Pricing

Territories (circle one)

    All territories

    Individual territories

_____

_____

_____

_____

_____

_____

Pricing & Royalty

    Primary Marketplace _____

    List Price Chosen _____ Currency ____

    Rate _____ Printing _____ Royalty _____

    Expanded Distribution?   Yes   No

    * Other Marketplace _____

    List Price Chosen _____ Currency ____

    Rate _____ Printing _____ Royalty _____

    * Other Marketplace _____

    List Price Chosen _____ Currency ____

    Rate _____ Printing _____ Royalty _____

    * Other Marketplace _____

    List Price Chosen _____ Currency ____

    Rate _____ Printing _____ Royalty _____

Book Title _____

* Other Marketplace _____

List Price Chosen _____ Currency ____

Rate _____ Printing _____ Royalty _____

* Other Marketplace _____

List Price Chosen _____ Currency ____

Rate _____ Printing _____ Royalty _____

* Other Marketplace _____

List Price Chosen _____ Currency ____

Rate _____ Printing _____ Royalty _____

Proof Copies

Requested a proof copy   Date _____

Arrival Date _____

Publication Status

Saved as Draft Date _____

Clicked Publish Button Date _____

Published Notice from KDP Date _____

Notes _____

_____

_____

_____

_____

_____

_____

_____

Book Title _____

Author Copy Orders

Date	#	Ship Speed	Ship Cost	Tax	Total	Arrived

Book Title _____

Note Date & Changes Made

_____

_____

_____

_____

_____

_____

_____

_____

_____

_____

_____

_____

_____

_____

_____

_____

_____

_____

_____

_____

_____

_____

_____

Book Title _____

Note Date & Changes Made

_____

_____

_____

_____

_____

_____

_____

_____

_____

_____

_____

_____

_____

_____

_____

_____

_____

_____

_____

_____

BOOK 16 - Date _____

Paperback Details

Language _____

Book Title _____

Subtitle _____

Series _____ # ____

Edition Number (if it applies) _____

Author _____

Contributors (if any) _____

_____

_____

_____

Description: _____

_____

_____

_____

_____

_____

_____

_____

_____

_____

_____

_____

_____

Publishing Rights (circle or underline one)

I own the copyright

This is a public domain work

Book Title _____

Keywords (seven words or phrases)

_____

_____

_____

_____

_____

_____

_____

Categories (two)

_____

_____

_____

Large Print   No Yes

Adult Content   No Yes

Paperback Content

Print ISBN (circle one)   Free KDP   My Own

ISBN _____

Imprint _____

Publication Date _____

Print Options circle one

Black & white interior with cream paper

Black & white interior with white paper

Color interior with white paper

Trim Size chosen: _____

Book Title _____

Bleed settings   No Bleed   Bleed

Paperback cover finish (circle one)   Matte   Glossy

Manuscript

File name _____

Uploaded   Date _____

Updated   Date _____

Updated   Date _____

Updated   Date _____

Interior Formatter _____

Contact Info: _____

Cost: _____

Book Cover

File name _____

Uploaded   Date _____

Updated   Date _____

Updated   Date _____

Updated   Date _____

Cover Designer _____

Contact Info: _____

Cost: _____

Book Preview - Approved Date _____

Downloaded a PDF Proof   Date _____

Summary

Page Count _____ Your Printing Cost _____

Notes _____

_____

Book Title _____

Paperback Rights & Pricing

Territories (circle one)

    All territories

    Individual territories

_____

_____

_____

_____

_____

_____

Pricing & Royalty

    Primary Marketplace _____

    List Price Chosen _____ Currency _____

    Rate _____ Printing _____ Royalty _____

    Expanded Distribution?   Yes   No

    * Other Marketplace _____

    List Price Chosen _____ Currency _____

    Rate _____ Printing _____ Royalty _____

    * Other Marketplace _____

    List Price Chosen _____ Currency _____

    Rate _____ Printing _____ Royalty _____

    * Other Marketplace _____

    List Price Chosen _____ Currency _____

    Rate _____ Printing _____ Royalty _____

Book Title _____

    * Other Marketplace _____

    List Price Chosen _____ Currency ____

    Rate _____ Printing _____ Royalty _____

    * Other Marketplace _____

    List Price Chosen _____ Currency ____

    Rate _____ Printing _____ Royalty _____

    * Other Marketplace _____

    List Price Chosen _____ Currency ____

    Rate _____ Printing _____ Royalty _____

Proof Copies

    Requested a proof copy   Date _____

    Arrival Date _____

Publication Status

    Saved as Draft Date _____

    Clicked Publish Button Date _____

    Published Notice from KDP Date _____

    Notes _____

    _____

    _____

    _____

    _____

    _____

    _____

    _____

Book Title _____

Author Copy Orders

Date	#	Ship Speed	Ship Cost	Tax	Total	Arrived

Book Title _____

Note Date & Changes Made

_____

_____

_____

_____

_____

_____

_____

_____

_____

_____

_____

_____

_____

_____

_____

_____

_____

_____

_____

_____

_____

_____

_____

_____

_____

Book Title _____

Note Date & Changes Made

_____
_____
_____
_____
_____
_____
_____
_____
_____
_____
_____
_____
_____
_____
_____
_____
_____
_____
_____
_____
_____
_____
_____
_____
_____

BOOK 17 - Date _____

Paperback Details

Language _____

Book Title _____

Subtitle _____

Series _____ # _____

Edition Number (if it applies) _____

Author _____

Contributors (if any) _____

_____

_____

_____

Description: _____

_____

_____

_____

_____

_____

_____

_____

_____

_____

_____

_____

_____

Publishing Rights (circle or underline one)

I own the copyright

This is a public domain work

Book Title _____

Keywords (seven words or phrases)

_____

_____

_____

_____

_____

_____

_____

Categories (two)

_____

_____

_____

Large Print   No Yes

Adult Content   No Yes

Paperback Content

Print ISBN (circle one)   Free KDP   My Own

   ISBN _____

   Imprint _____

   Publication Date _____

Print Options circle one

   Black & white interior with cream paper

   Black & white interior with white paper

   Color interior with white paper

   Trim Size chosen: _____

Book Title _____

    Bleed settings   No Bleed   Bleed

    Paperback cover finish (circle one)   Matte   Glossy

Manuscript

    File name _____

    Uploaded   Date _____

    Updated   Date _____

    Updated   Date _____

    Updated   Date _____

    Interior Formatter _____

    Contact Info: _____

    Cost: _____

Book Cover

    File name _____

    Uploaded   Date _____

    Updated   Date _____

    Updated   Date _____

    Updated   Date _____

    Cover Designer _____

    Contact Info: _____

    Cost: _____

Book Preview - Approved Date _____

    Downloaded a PDF Proof   Date _____

Summary

    Page Count _____ Your Printing Cost _____

    Notes _____

    _____

Book Title _____

Paperback Rights & Pricing

Territories (circle one)

    All territories

    Individual territories

_____

_____

_____

_____

_____

_____

Pricing & Royalty

    Primary Marketplace _____

    List Price Chosen _____ Currency _____

    Rate _____ Printing _____ Royalty _____

    Expanded Distribution?   Yes   No

    * Other Marketplace _____

    List Price Chosen _____ Currency _____

    Rate _____ Printing _____ Royalty _____

    * Other Marketplace _____

    List Price Chosen _____ Currency _____

    Rate _____ Printing _____ Royalty _____

    * Other Marketplace _____

    List Price Chosen _____ Currency _____

    Rate _____ Printing _____ Royalty _____

Book Title _____

* Other Marketplace _____

List Price Chosen _____ Currency _____

Rate _____ Printing _____ Royalty _____

* Other Marketplace _____

List Price Chosen _____ Currency _____

Rate _____ Printing _____ Royalty _____

* Other Marketplace _____

List Price Chosen _____ Currency _____

Rate _____ Printing _____ Royalty _____

Proof Copies

Requested a proof copy   Date _____

Arrival Date _____

Publication Status

Saved as Draft Date _____

Clicked Publish Button Date _____

Published Notice from KDP Date _____

Notes _____

_____

_____

_____

_____

_____

_____

_____

Book Title _____

Author Copy Orders

Date   #   Ship Speed   Ship Cost   Tax   Total   Arrived

_____

_____

_____

_____

_____

_____

_____

_____

_____

_____

_____

_____

_____

_____

_____

_____

_____

_____

_____

_____

Book Title _____

Note Date & Changes Made

_____

_____

_____

_____

_____

_____

_____

_____

_____

_____

_____

_____

_____

_____

_____

_____

_____

_____

_____

_____

_____

_____

_____

_____

Book Title _____

Note Date & Changes Made

_____
_____
_____
_____
_____
_____
_____
_____
_____
_____
_____
_____
_____
_____
_____
_____
_____
_____
_____
_____
_____
_____
_____
_____
_____
_____

BOOK 18 - Date _____

Paperback Details

Language _____

Book Title _____

Subtitle _____

Series _____ # _____

Edition Number (if it applies) _____

Author _____

Contributors (if any) _____

_____

_____

_____

Description: _____

_____

_____

_____

_____

_____

_____

_____

_____

_____

_____

_____

_____

Publishing Rights (circle or underline one)

I own the copyright

This is a public domain work

Book Title _____

Keywords (seven words or phrases)

_____

_____

_____

_____

_____

_____

_____

Categories (two)

_____

_____

_____

Large Print   No Yes

Adult Content   No Yes

Paperback Content

Print ISBN (circle one)   Free KDP   My Own

   ISBN _____

   Imprint _____

   Publication Date _____

Print Options circle one

   Black & white interior with cream paper

   Black & white interior with white paper

   Color interior with white paper

   Trim Size chosen: _____

Book Title _____

    Bleed settings   No Bleed Bleed

    Paperback cover finish (circle one)   Matte   Glossy

Manuscript

    File name _____

    Uploaded   Date _____

    Updated   Date _____

    Updated   Date _____

    Updated   Date _____

    Interior Formatter _____

    Contact Info: _____

    Cost: _____

Book Cover

    File name _____

    Uploaded   Date _____

    Updated   Date _____

    Updated   Date _____

    Updated   Date _____

    Cover Designer _____

    Contact Info: _____

    Cost: _____

Book Preview - Approved Date _____

    Downloaded a PDF Proof   Date _____

Summary

    Page Count _____ Your Printing Cost _____

    Notes _____

    _____

Book Title _____

Paperback Rights & Pricing

Territories (circle one)

    All territories

    Individual territories

_____

_____

_____

_____

_____

_____

Pricing & Royalty

    Primary Marketplace _____

    List Price Chosen _____ Currency ____

    Rate _____ Printing _____ Royalty _____

    Expanded Distribution?   Yes   No

    * Other Marketplace _____

    List Price Chosen _____ Currency ____

    Rate _____ Printing _____ Royalty _____

    * Other Marketplace _____

    List Price Chosen _____ Currency ____

    Rate _____ Printing _____ Royalty _____

    * Other Marketplace _____

    List Price Chosen _____ Currency ____

    Rate _____ Printing _____ Royalty _____

Book Title _____

  * Other Marketplace _____

  List Price Chosen _____ Currency _____

  Rate _____ Printing _____ Royalty _____

  * Other Marketplace _____

  List Price Chosen _____ Currency _____

  Rate _____ Printing _____ Royalty _____

  * Other Marketplace _____

  List Price Chosen _____ Currency _____

  Rate _____ Printing _____ Royalty _____

Proof Copies

  Requested a proof copy Date _____

  Arrival Date _____

Publication Status

  Saved as Draft Date _____

  Clicked Publish Button Date _____

  Published Notice from KDP Date _____

  Notes _____

  _____

  _____

  _____

  _____

  _____

  _____

  _____

Book Title _____

Author Copy Orders

Date	#	Ship Speed	Ship Cost	Tax	Total	Arrived

Book Title _____

Note Date & Changes Made

_____

_____

_____

_____

_____

_____

_____

_____

_____

_____

_____

_____

_____

_____

_____

_____

_____

_____

_____

_____

_____

_____

_____

Book Title _____

Note Date & Changes Made

_____

_____

_____

_____

_____

_____

_____

_____

_____

_____

_____

_____

_____

_____

_____

_____

_____

_____

_____

_____

_____

_____

_____

BOOK 19 - Date _____

Paperback Details

Language _____

Book Title _____

Subtitle _____

Series _____ # ____

Edition Number (if it applies) _____

Author _____

Contributors (if any) _____

_____

_____

_____

Description: _____

_____

_____

_____

_____

_____

_____

_____

_____

_____

_____

_____

Publishing Rights (circle or underline one)

      I own the copyright

      This is a public domain work

Book Title _____

Keywords (seven words or phrases)

_____

_____

_____

_____

_____

_____

_____

Categories (two)

_____

_____

_____

_____

Large Print   No Yes

Adult Content   No Yes

Paperback Content

Print ISBN (circle one)   Free KDP   My Own

ISBN _____

Imprint _____

Publication Date _____

Print Options circle one

Black & white interior with cream paper

Black & white interior with white paper

Color interior with white paper

Trim Size chosen: _____

Book Title _____

Bleed settings   No Bleed   Bleed

Paperback cover finish (circle one)   Matte   Glossy

Manuscript

File name _____

Uploaded   Date _____

Updated   Date _____

Updated   Date _____

Updated   Date _____

Interior Formatter _____

Contact Info: _____

Cost: _____

Book Cover

File name _____

Uploaded   Date _____

Updated   Date _____

Updated   Date _____

Updated   Date _____

Cover Designer _____

Contact Info: _____

Cost: _____

Book Preview - Approved Date _____

Downloaded a PDF Proof   Date _____

Summary

Page Count _____ Your Printing Cost _____

Notes _____

_____

Book Title _____

Paperback Rights & Pricing

Territories (circle one)

    All territories

    Individual territories

_____

_____

_____

_____

_____

_____

Pricing & Royalty

    Primary Marketplace _____

    List Price Chosen _____ Currency _____

    Rate _____ Printing _____ Royalty _____

    Expanded Distribution?   Yes   No

    * Other Marketplace _____

    List Price Chosen _____ Currency _____

    Rate _____ Printing _____ Royalty _____

    * Other Marketplace _____

    List Price Chosen _____ Currency _____

    Rate _____ Printing _____ Royalty _____

    * Other Marketplace _____

    List Price Chosen _____ Currency _____

    Rate _____ Printing _____ Royalty _____

Book Title _____

     * Other Marketplace _____

     List Price Chosen _____ Currency _____

     Rate _____ Printing _____ Royalty _____

     * Other Marketplace _____

     List Price Chosen _____ Currency _____

     Rate _____ Printing _____ Royalty _____

     * Other Marketplace _____

     List Price Chosen _____ Currency _____

     Rate _____ Printing _____ Royalty _____

Proof Copies

     Requested a proof copy   Date _____

     Arrival Date _____

Publication Status

     Saved as Draft Date _____

     Clicked Publish Button Date _____

     Published Notice from KDP Date _____

     Notes _____

     _____

     _____

     _____

     _____

     _____

     _____

     _____

Book Title _____

Author Copy Orders

Date	#	Ship Speed	Ship Cost	Tax	Total	Arrived

Book Title _____

Note Date & Changes Made

_____

_____

_____

_____

_____

_____

_____

_____

_____

_____

_____

_____

_____

_____

_____

_____

_____

_____

_____

_____

_____

_____

_____

Book Title _____

Note Date & Changes Made

_____

_____

_____

_____

_____

_____

_____

_____

_____

_____

_____

_____

_____

_____

_____

_____

_____

_____

_____

_____

_____

_____

_____

_____

BOOK 20 - Date _____

Paperback Details

Language _____

Book Title _____

Subtitle _____

Series _____ # ____

Edition Number (if it applies) _____

Author _____

Contributors (if any) _____

_____

_____

_____

Description: _____

_____

_____

_____

_____

_____

_____

_____

_____

_____

_____

_____

_____

Publishing Rights (circle or underline one)

I own the copyright

This is a public domain work

Book Title _____

Keywords (seven words or phrases)

_____

_____

_____

_____

_____

_____

_____

Categories (two)

_____

_____

_____

Large Print   No Yes

Adult Content   No Yes

Paperback Content

Print ISBN (circle one)   Free KDP   My Own

ISBN _____

Imprint _____

Publication Date _____

Print Options circle one

Black & white interior with cream paper

Black & white interior with white paper

Color interior with white paper

Trim Size chosen: _____

Book Title _____

Bleed settings   No Bleed   Bleed

Paperback cover finish (circle one)   Matte   Glossy

Manuscript

File name _____

Uploaded   Date _____

Updated   Date _____

Updated   Date _____

Updated   Date _____

Interior Formatter _____

Contact Info: _____

Cost: _____

Book Cover

File name _____

Uploaded   Date _____

Updated   Date _____

Updated   Date _____

Updated   Date _____

Cover Designer _____

Contact Info: _____

Cost: _____

Book Preview - Approved Date _____

Downloaded a PDF Proof   Date _____

Summary

Page Count _____ Your Printing Cost _____

Notes _____

_____

Book Title _____

Paperback Rights & Pricing

Territories (circle one)

    All territories

    Individual territories

_____

_____

_____

_____

_____

_____

Pricing & Royalty

    Primary Marketplace _____

    List Price Chosen _____ Currency ____

    Rate _____ Printing _____ Royalty _____

    Expanded Distribution?   Yes   No

    * Other Marketplace _____

    List Price Chosen _____ Currency ____

    Rate _____ Printing _____ Royalty _____

    * Other Marketplace _____

    List Price Chosen _____ Currency ____

    Rate _____ Printing _____ Royalty _____

    * Other Marketplace _____

    List Price Chosen _____ Currency ____

    Rate _____ Printing _____ Royalty _____

Book Title _____

* Other Marketplace _____

List Price Chosen _____ Currency _____

Rate _____ Printing _____ Royalty _____

* Other Marketplace _____

List Price Chosen _____ Currency _____

Rate _____ Printing _____ Royalty _____

* Other Marketplace _____

List Price Chosen _____ Currency _____

Rate _____ Printing _____ Royalty _____

Proof Copies

Requested a proof copy   Date _____

Arrival Date _____

Publication Status

Saved as Draft Date _____

Clicked Publish Button Date _____

Published Notice from KDP Date _____

Notes _____

_____

_____

_____

_____

_____

_____

_____

Book Title _____

Author Copy Orders

Date	#	Ship Speed	Ship Cost	Tax	Total	Arrived

Book Title _____

Note Date & Changes Made

_____

_____

_____

_____

_____

_____

_____

_____

_____

_____

_____

_____

_____

_____

_____

_____

_____

_____

_____

_____

_____

_____

_____

_____

Book Title _____

Note Date & Changes Made

About the Creator of
WestWard Journals

Marsha Ward writes authentic historical fiction, and nonfiction having to do with writing. Her novels include The Owen Family Saga series, the Shenandoah Neighbors series, and many other works of fiction. Her nonfiction books include *The Checklist: Indie Publishing My Way, Rapid Recipes for Writers . . . And Other Busy People,* and *From Julia's Kitchen: Owen Family Cookery.*

Find her online at Amazon or at marshaward.com.

www.ingramcontent.com/pod-product-compliance
Lightning Source LLC
Chambersburg PA
CBHW050528280326
41933CB00031B/1264